LINES

OF

DEFENSE

LINES

OF

DEFENSE

poems

STEPHEN DUNN

W. W. NORTON & COMPANY

NEW YORK · LONDON

Epigraph from *This Business of Living: Diaries, 1935–1950* by Cesare Pavese.
Copyright © 2009 by Aldine Publishers. Reprinted by permission of
Aldine Transaction, a division of Transaction Publishers.

For information about permission to reproduce selections from this book,
write to Permissions, W. W. Norton & Company, Inc.,
500 Fifth Avenue, New York, NY 10110

For information about special discounts for bulk purchases, please contact
W. W. Norton Special Sales at specialsales@wwnorton.com or 800-233-4830

Manufacturing by Courier Westford
Production manager: Louise Mattarelliano

Library of Congress Cataloging-in-Publication Data

Dunn, Stephen, date.
[Poems. Selections]
Lines of Defense : poems / Stephen Dunn. — First Edition.
pages cm
ISBN 978-0-393-24081-8 (hardcover)
I. Title.
PS3554.U49A6 2014
811'.54—dc23
                          2013029488

W. W. Norton & Company, Inc.
500 Fifth Avenue, New York, N.Y. 10110
www.wwnorton.com

W. W. Norton & Company Ltd.
Castle House, 75/76 Wells Street, London W1T 3QT

1 2 3 4 5 6 7 8 9 0

For Lawrence Raab & Jonathan Aaron

Literature is a defense against the attacks of life.

—CESARE PAVESE

CONTENTS

IV

ACKNOWLEDGMENTS

The following poems were published or are about to be
published in these journals:

The American Poetry Review: "Delicacies," "Formalities
for the Long Road," "Maggie and the Gauchos," "For
the Player," "The Man with Three Horses," "The
Widening," "The Proliferation," "Odds Are," "Old Past,
Near Past," "Cleaning Up," "Nothing to Hold Onto"
Boston Review: "For My Son"
The Georgia Review: "The Statue of Responsibility," "Before
We Leave"
Green Mountains Review: "Ache"
Harvard Review: "Intrusions"
The Kenyon Review: "The Obvious"
New Letters: "Their Loneliness"
The New Yorker: "Reconstruction," "Testimony," "The Party
to Which You Are Not Invited"
The Paris Review: "Sea Level," "Feathers"
Parnassus: "If the Poet"
Plume: "Another Argument with Jim About the Soul"
Poetry: "In Love, His Grammar Grew"
The Southern Review: "Anniversary Poem," "In Another
Country," "Letter to the Man I Once Was"
Shenandoah: "Thank You," "Out of Respect"
Smithsonian: "The Chicken and the Egg"
TriQuarterly: "A Coldness," "The Little Details," "Those
Without Final Residence"

"The Statue of Responsibility" was chosen for *The Best American Poetry 2013*

Many thanks to Yaddo and The MacDowell Colony for residencies at which many of these poems were begun, and sometimes concluded, if not finished.

I

It Was a Time

Some of us just wanted to drop out, go far away
from integrity's demands. Others sought strange
consultations with their almost vanished selves.
And the brave, they would meet somewhere
in zero weather to subvert the drift of the land.
It was a time to link arms, or cross the border.
And who were you, and who was I?
Such questions seemed like a lifelong job.
We put the world on notice, and the world
hardly noticed. When we occupied the offices

of people who just wanted to do their jobs
and go home, we thought we'd done something
historical, bold. We desired to be as compelling
as Belmondo with a cigarette, Monica Vitti
looking just so. But always the familiar banalities
would return—an existential day followed
by a comfortable night, the rhapsodies
of achievement, then a great smalling down.
No one could be sure what was true. In time
we became people we only occasionally knew.

BEFORE WE LEAVE

Just so it's clear—
no whining on the journey.
If you whine, you'll get stuck
somewhere with people
like yourself. It's an unwritten law.
Wear hiking boots. Pack food
and a change of clothes.
We go slowly. Endurance won't
be enough, though without it
you can't get to the place
where more of you is asked.
Expect there will be times
when you'll be afraid.
Hold hands and tremble together
if you must but remember
each of you is alone.

Where are we going?
It's not an issue of here or there.
And if you ever feel you can't
take another step, imagine
how you might feel to arrive,
if not wiser, a little more aware
how to inhabit the middle ground
between misery and joy.
Trudge on. In the higher regions,
where the footing is unsure,
to trudge is to survive.

Happiness is another journey,
almost over before it starts,
guaranteed to disappoint.
If you've come for it, say so,
you'll get your money back.
I hope you all realize that anytime
is a fine time to laugh. Fake it,
however, and false laughter
will accompany you like a cowbell
for the rest of your days.
You'll forever lack the seriousness
of a clown. At some point
the rocks will be jagged,
the precipice sheer. That won't be
the abyss you'll see, looking down.
The abyss, you'll discover
(if you've made it this far),
is usually nearer than that—
at the bottom of something
you've yet to resolve,
or posing as your confidante.
Follow me. Don't follow me. I will
say such things, and mean both.

THE COUNTRY OF THE NEXT THING

The border guards to the fictional country have fallen asleep.
Still, dangers exist. You've brought bones for their dogs
who are curiously friendly, which means there's a chance
you may be safe because you've learned to be wary
of any creatures that remind you of how you might behave
if trained to perceive sweetness as a ruse, a strategy.
This fictional country is *your* baby, as it were,
and you have most possibilities covered.
If the guards were to awaken, you know they prefer
bribes over bullets, which is why you've recently emptied
one of your Swiss bank accounts, prepared, as ever, for avarice.
This is a country famous for its crossroads, and you're the kind
of traveler who thrives on decisions. At the juncture of
The End Is Near and Everything This Way Is Forbidden
you take the road invisible to all
but fictionists, strewn with now-you-see-them,
now-you-don't pleasures, and the skeletons of critics.
You make sure that all the hitchhikers on this road possess
ribald tales of adventure. *Oh faux darlings of my dreamworld,*
you say to yourself, *come sit in the passenger seat, and complete
for me my narrative.* But soon there are more signs
that promise Turns this way, Punishments the other.
This is when you invent the characters capable of dealing
with misfortune, or those destined to go wrong because
you haven't given them imagination. Remember, all of them
are you. So be careful. Ahead of you are the usual tears
and lamentations, the various comedies of the next thing.

TRACKS

In their dark hovels,
places where there's no separating
a criminal from someone unlucky,
or a smart-ass from an aspiring artist,
shadow boys were breaking
all the laws, and girls with spray cans
felt a permission to create
colorful doorways and skylights
on the white, confining walls.
What's one to do who has no money
and a hatred of other people's rules?
A leather jacket helped for some,
and for others a neckline that promised
a descent into a dreamland,
but did not solve the problems
of having parents too busy to care,
and a police force charged to serve
the strict quiescence of the status quo.
The girls kept mistaking mascara
for a way of hiding, a few of the boys
a knife for a persuasive argument.
Finally, someone grown up, but with
shadow-boy credentials and a sweet
toughness that gave him authority, said
Cut that shit out, and the boys and girls
tried for maybe a week. But it was a small town,
and everyone knew options belonged
to the rich with their houses on the hill.

Let's steal a Lexus, one of the boys said.
Let's take it for a wild ride, and Yes,
let's paint it piss-yellow, said the girl alive
with anger. Let's break a few windows, too.
And the man with the credentials,
as if suddenly remembering the viscera
of his past, got quiet, realized nothing
he would say could compete with how good
self-destruction sometimes feels.

Cleaning Up

Trying to learn after all these years
to be gracious, sorrow-freed,
at least a decade beyond the old rut
of needless suffering, I imagine

joining hands with a young Nadezhda
Mandelstam and an aging Nelson Mandela,
and be done with those greats
as well as the difficulties they triumphed over.

I don't want to be brave, or safe.
I resolve never to fake joy,
or pursue old grief. If I encounter opacity,
I'll try to smash it with something clear.

I have no nostalgia for a landscape,
in spite of how much there is to retrieve.
And I'll keep to myself how I want
to reveal a few secrets that will unlock

the faraway, the unknown. No point
in saying what your enemies can use
when you fail. If offered it, even as a lark,
I don't want immortality, the boredom

of living on. But for the work, sure.
Please don't ask, Who cares what you want?
I don't want to have to say my name.
On occasion someone gives me

something wonderful, like a kiss
or a ticket to a place
that doesn't exist until I arrive,
and I'm not going to complain

that I'm not sure why. And some days
I'm content to play city games
like betting on when a light will change,
or if a woman might emerge from a manhole

in the street. If weather encroaches, I'll go
inside, take down a romance from the shelf.
Mostly, though, I want nothing that might
require me to want what I can't have.

Let someone else open the mail,
hopefully. I'm in the mood to clean,
to keep what I can. Every day, if I could,
I'd oppose history by altering one detail.

Thank You,

dear, for taking our granddaughter Samantha
to the carnival, and then to the park
with monkey bars and swings.
I haven't been lemurlike for years,
and I no longer wish to push kids toward heaven,
even if they swing back to earth
fascinated and unchurchly—as I wish
them to be. Samantha believes in monsters
both good and bad, sweet things
with strange hungers. Keep this in mind
when at the carnival you introduce her
to the fun house meant to distort and please.
Try to smile at how grotesque you become,
and, for my sake, tell her her grandfather
is always looking for mirrors that give back
something other than himself. I'd tell her
myself, but I'm happily here, hiding out
in our house where today the fun for me
is not going to any carnival or park.
So smart of you to leave me behind.
I would have lagged with lack of interest,
perhaps declared one or two alienable rights.
Thank you for knowing my tendencies,
which are not to be admired, I realize,
though I love that you honor them
some of the time. When Samantha grows up,
doing for herself what she has learned
from me, let's hope someone like you

understands monkey business trumps duty
most days of the week. Is that true?—
a voice cannot help but ask.
Thank you anyway for taking her
to these places where other children gather,
and enjoy themselves so fully it seems
they never wonder why their grandfathers
are elsewhere. But that same voice says,
doesn't every heart have a ledger,
isn't every absence an event to be recorded?

NOTHING TO HOLD ONTO

When it's time to enter the great waters,
you, who've been properly loved since birth,
will likely feel on top of the world,
lacking the useful defenses the unloved have.

Try to remember that *on top of the world*
is only an expression, nothing to hold onto,
and if there were such a place,
no doubt there'd be a host of angels

who might think it their territory.
You would need to be careful
of the jealous, bitter ones
who haven't gotten the best assignments.

It might be the right time to cultivate
disbelief, which can make certain angels
disappear. Actually, disbelief is always useful,
helps the discriminate discriminate.

Those of you properly loved will believe
your biggest mistakes can be overcome.
You will have learned laughter
is a floatation device, and uproarious laughter

the password to moments of fine feeling.
It means the angel assigned to you at birth,
the only one you believe in, has already wrapped
his wings around you, is doing his job.

Still, there'll be turbulence as you enter
the great waters. Love alone can't save you,
and disbelief only frees you long enough
to see clearly where you're going.

But the loved have a history of shifting
as the world shifts, and a vague sense
how good and bad blend, become one.
Don't worry if you can't tell the angelic

from the hellbent, or the exact meaning of guidance.
Confusion won't hurt you. This is your chance
to row as hard as the unloved, whose task
from the beginning was to exceed all expectations.

SOMETHING NEEDED TO BE DONE

for B.

I've tried to believe the ancient Greeks
were wrong: you *can* count yourself happy
before the final verdict is in.

Let's bring in the Chorus for a song.

The kings and queens knew what they excreted
would make it down to us; it was the nature,
the gravity of things. So in the low places

happiness was a triumph
of engineering and ingenuity,
the very things the Chorus recommended

practicing—until practicing became an art.
We'd hear their mellifluous tones
amid the ambiguities of dawn,

the slate gray middle ground of dusk.
Who were they, really? The community?
A group of wise friends?

They seemed to understand
that you were beautiful,
and that beauty leaves us little choice.

We heard what we wanted to hear,
as the Greeks at Delphi did.
Something was telling us

something needed to be done.

The moon was full of itself.
I was doomed to feel its pull.
I had nightmares. I had mere dreams

full of cravings and scatological talk.
I worried about overly tidy men
who didn't know until too late

that it was their mothers they wanted.
The Greeks had it down all right.
I was sure, my sweet, I wasn't one of them.

The Chorus began to sing: *the fewer
the words the more they are felt.*
It was 2013, and words were

sprawling all over the place. If they named
what had to be done, they named
too much. No longer were there hints

hidden in the spaces at the end
of a line or a wish. My smartest friend
said if I wanted illumination

I'd have to learn to love the shadows
it creates. He said maybe
it isn't enough to love just one person.

You are beautiful, he said,
but so was Helen, and how different
the world would be if men like Paris

loved hundreds instead of one.
Troublemaker, troublemaker,
the Chorus sang, wanting as ever

for things to be better than they are.

Here in Garrett County we've all
been getting fat. It saves us from the perils
of attractiveness. When the rains come

we don't try to call out to Poseidon.
Most here believe in one God, and ask Him
to bless only us. I love you, my love.

I feel happy today, though I know today
is just a speck in time. Is that our song
the Chorus is singing? Or is it the wind

in the hemlocks, preceding a storm?

NOW, FINALLY

Homage to a late-in-life-marriage—
for Philip

Now, finally, a matter of something else,
the delusions of choosing
behind each of you, and those people
you married or didn't marry
also behind you,
because you knew too little
about love, or counted on it too much

as if love could ever be enough,

though without it, no hope, no renewals
when the disappointments come,
no passage through the kitchen slop
the boredom and the bills
to some higher regard.

I've seen that good glow
emanating unfakable,

but the past won't wholly disappear,
it can't,
you're everything you've ever done,
everyone you've known,

and for a while, yes, everything, everyone,
gets into bed with you. It's dark
under the covers and it's warm.
Hold on to each other—those others
will go their ghostly ways.

ANNIVERSARY POEM

Remember that day in the rain
at the park where we used to meet,

how we took and we gave,
and what couldn't be spoken

was nevertheless contained
in what we were able to say,

well, it's raining again
and it's the body, I realize,

that stores memory
and sends it, when keyed,

to those long unvisited
regions of the brain—remember

that steady collision
of rain and branch and leaf,

a hundred connections
happening at once,

long before I said *I do.*
I was saying *I will* and *Let's.*

INTRUSIONS

The narcissists, as ever, were rhyming themselves
with themselves, while a few houses away,
a man with a certain urgency, but with no
philosophical position on the matter,
wanted early-morning sex

more than did his wife. She wasn't a prude.
She just liked to be wooed
before being pinned down, wanted her eyes
more than half open, didn't want
to feel like some opening act.

It was clear an ape lived somewhere
in the man's past, and could—at the right time—
be seen in the woman's behavior, too,
though the DNA of those small, fuck-crazy-
any-time-any-which-way bonobos

had been civilized out of her, or so it seemed.
Otherwise, she had efficient opposable thumbs,
and a desire to please him when she wasn't awakened
by a pressing issue not hers. One day the narcissists
dropped by uninvited just after dinner to offer

the importance of their presence. The man and woman
had been talking, taking turns, as it were, about why
she preferred something else to the Anglo-Saxon words
he used to further arouse her into wakefulness.
They allowed their visitors to overhear the act

of thinking inside and outside a subject, because, after all,
the subject was intrusion, its niceties and violations,
and their neighbors were part of it now,
who had come wishing to *communicate*—that big word
certain people use who have no gift for it.

If you want it to last it's important
to get off to a good start. Don't let
a ship's captain marry you
unless he's adept at changing course.
Don't let any dogma have its day.
No doubt, though, society will want
some kind of priest to officiate.
Say the words you must say,
but be sure to violate all the stupid stuff.
Or why not hire someone, say twelve credits
short of being an expert, who can sing
and knows something about serious fun?

After the ceremony, change into that funky
outfit that drives only the right men crazy.
Hope your husband will be one of them.
Heed the intelligence of outright lust.
But invite those women friends it drives crazy, too.
Always anticipate a *just in case* scenario.
Make reservations at an Indonesian
French restaurant whose specialty is call Pleasure-
for-More-Than-One. Speak your best velvety French.

Tell your man one of your fantasies is taking off
a cummerbund while pronouncing its name.
Recommend he keep his on for a while.
Tell him also you have nothing
against God, but remember only an insecure God,

like an insecure man, insists that a woman
must obey. Remind him that all the Bible
stories were written by men. Your job now
is to define what heavenly is, and heaven itself,
and find ways to let him in.

In Love, His Grammar Grew

In love, his grammar grew
rich with intensifiers, and adverbs fell
madly from the sky like pheasants
for the peasantry, and he, as sated
as they were, lolled under shade trees
until roused by moonlight
and the beautiful fraternal twins
and and *but*. Oh that was when
he knew he couldn't resist
a conjunction of any kind.
One said *accumulate*, the other
was a doubter who loved the wind
and the mind that cleans up after it.
                              For love
he wanted to break all the rules,
light a candle behind a sentence
named Sheila, always running on
and wishing to be stopped
by the hard button of a period.
Sometimes, in desperation, he'd look
toward a mannequin or a window dresser
with a penchant for parsing.
But mostly he wanted you, Sheila,
and the adjectives that could precede
and change you: *bluesy, fly-by-night,*
queen of all that is and might be.

Formalities for the Long Road

I used to think, Let's take a jet or a Harley
to where we need to go. Let's take a car
with five on the floor. I used to think *sooner*
would always give us a better chance.

Now it seems we should take our time,
look at ourselves, and try to maintain a pace
that keeps us even, or in the vicinity of
what we care about. My love, you know

it's difficult for me these days to be
a public man—shakey hands, hobbled gait.
Don't let me hide. You know that racetrack
where no one races anymore,

where it's impossible to lose or win—
I'll be waiting inside by the finish line.
Come get me, and let's leave from there.
I know there's no straight road ahead.

If the ugliness along the way
begins to disturb—fumes
in the air, slime by the curb,
the mean-spirited tenor of the land—

let's realize we'll not get through
unsmirched or unscathed. The road
will only get darker as we go,
and nothing's pure. But white lines

are there to help show the way,
and signs to guide and warn, formalities
I trust won't entirely keep us
from a little recklessness.

Theory says there's some comfort
if many of us are in the same mess.
So let's bring the van
and invite our friends, and hope

for the best before the road dips
and fog begins. Let's see if we can toast
to what we've become.
Purely, dear, is how I'd like to hold

you then—all the little tarnished things
time has had its way with
boxed and labeled
and with us until the end.

II

IF THE POET

If the poet doesn't yield to the priest,
as Stevens says he shouldn't,
and if both reside in the same village,
and call on their powers to rectify
or explain the latest disaster,

does the priest become less persuasive
because his ideas are likely not his own,
and is the poet suspect for the same reason?
Would a good priest find the right words,
as the good poet would, in among the many words

passed down for centuries
on what to think, what to believe?
Or would reverence
always get in the way of the true,
thus possibly giving the poet the edge?

That is, if the poet mistrusts words, as he should,
makes them pass hard tests, knows they must
be arranged and shaped in order to convey
even a smidgen of truth, wouldn't he,
although self-ordained, be more reliable?

But what if the villagers believed
they were saved by a prayer the priest said
one Sunday among the ruins? And all the poet
could do was elegize the ruins?
Would the real and the imagined fuse,
become something entirely new?

And what if the poet and priest were one,
each invoking the other as the crops grew
and rain was steady in rainy season, or,
just as confusing, things got worse
and prayers proved useless, and poems
merely decorated the debris where a house

once was? Would it be time for the priest
to admit he'd known but one book? For the poet
to say he'd read many, and look, it hasn't helped?
Or has the issue from the start been a great need
that can't be fully met, only made bearable
and sometimes served by those who try?

III

THE LITTLE DETAILS

The ice maker in his house is stuck, he says,
a little piece of ice jamming the opening,
and I tell him that earthquake in Arezzo
was close to where I vacationed last year
when the world was Tuscan and good.
My brother is talking about his ice maker
because a man can't talk about his lymphoma
and chemo every minute of the day.
And the earthquake—I think he knows—
is my way of speaking about a situation
not his, a different kind of unfairness.
Besides, what's a life without its little details—
trips to the market, a good parking spot.
He has to hang up, has a bet on the Jets-
Patriots game, which is about to start.
He's sure the Jets will cover the spread.
I make the opposite bet, our old fun.
Later, I put on my Maria Callas CD,
full of words I don't understand, but do.
If your brother has cancer, how lucky
to find someone to sing you beyond
what you've permitted yourself to feel.
Last time he visited he shrugged, smiled,
threw up his hands, as if to say
he was implicated in the big comedy now.
Then we played a card game called Push
and drank fine scotch, and turned on the TV.

THOSE WITHOUT FINAL RESIDENCE

roam between the bed and the closet.
Whatever in life they were deprived of
they try to claim as theirs.

There's rarely a skeleton in a closet
that doesn't want to don our clothes,
get out for a romp or a stroll.

We may think we see them
in our dreams, walking some boulevard
dressed as father, mother, mistress.

But all we can really see is the broom
as it sweeps things
under the rug. The ghosts themselves

aren't visible, at most offer glimpses,
and speak, if they speak at all,
in a language that only resembles ours.

The bed is not a resting place for them.
They are uncomfortable wherever
we have found ease. Many wish to tell us this

in the form of a sudden wind, or dip
in temperature, to rouse us
from our idle pleasantries.

Some of course commute quietly,
not wishing to disturb. The bed won't let them
under its covers. The closet says, Lie down

among the shoes and the fallen hangers.
It's not their fault that we sense
their presences, feel their spidery traces.

RECONSTRUCTION

The volcanoes, once so active,
are mostly quiet now, my friend says,
no way of telling us what they know.
And the dinosaurs, bone by bone,
may have been reconstructed,
but their stories, too, largely remain
untold, their skulls most likely full,
he says—like prehistoric black boxes—
of high-pitched, indecipherable screams.
All the theories are wrong
about what went wrong, my friend insists,
famous for being more interesting
than right. He says the volcanoes
helped the dinosaurs thrive
in the lowlands. On a tablecloth in ink
he re-creates the scene—a topography
of little volcanic disturbances
that kept Tyrannosaurus rex
and other big nuisances in check.
And then there was a turning point,
he says, a matter of vegetation
and scarcity and greed. An old story,
he calls it, as if simply affirming a fact—
the dinosaurs, when it came to food,
never knew how much was too much,
and given the size of their brains
kept doing a lot of almost forgivable
stupid things. But he's heard himself,

and seemingly amused is quick
to point out that forgiveness
wasn't even a concept yet, or a word,
still eons away from
a certain slithering and the likes of us.

ARCHAEOLOGY

I tell you nothing new when I say
here we are again, unable to claim
many moments of relief
from the confirmable gloom, though
there was a time, before news became
ubiquitous, when it was possible
to close our eyes and hide in our rooms.
The excitement of bones found
in mass graves—not ours—the remains
of mastodons and dinosaurs, told us
something of our past. Now we see
face down in ditches our neighbors
with whom we once broke bread,
whose children played in our yards,
and everywhere colossal denials of blame.
I tell you nothing new, Andre. I dare
boring you, Miguel, with what
you already know, the enemy
suddenly the enemy, *down on your knees,*
motherfucker, for being down on
your knees to the wrong god.
I dare boring you because the shovels
are blades, the dirt is bloody, and I need
to remind myself of the creatures
we are and have been—remnants
everywhere, no need, really, to dig.

You say I'd know it exists if
I were someone who had experienced
those inner brushfires that arise
without warning, and who loves
a good rampage now and then,
and even the weary solitude
that might follow it.
                    Perhaps,
but I believe the soul exists, too.
Mine is a ravenous thing
when it's awake. But mostly it sleeps,
waiting to be nudged, pricked, startled.

Around this time we invoke a thinker—
you, Emerson—me, Novalis—
to bolster the weakness of our thinking.

        You offer another example—
I'm not sure of what—of an old love
knocking on your door as if a miracle
had occurred, and say, "As St. John
of the Cross says, my dog called Ego
had gotten off its leash."
Then you swear a rope ladder
suddenly dropped from the clouds,
and an angel descended
proclaiming the end of celestial lies.
      I stop you there, and say

that saddens me because celestial lies
are my favorite lies, but what does that
have to do with soul? Rather than being
miraculous or grand, my soul
is more like a night janitor
nodding off on the job, unaware he's
waiting to be made alert by dawn.

When I cite Wittgenstein, and a passage
from Bertrand Russell to prove my point,
I think you cannot help but assent.

                You're a pain in the ass,
you say instead, I'm talking fire here,
I'm talking rampage and old loves,
and you're talking about this little dead,
sleepy thing wearing overalls.
                        I know I'm wrong
to mock anyone's sense of the unknown,
but I say, Look, the soul is a white ball
of slop, and attribute it to Nietzsche.
Blazing ball of fire! Fucking blazing ball
of fire! you scream, as if you know
the quote and are correcting me.

THEIR LONELINESS

Having a child with two heads, each with a brain,
made the parents aware that intelligence
was dispensed unfairly in this world.

The head they named John could theorize,
particularly concerning the notion
that two might not be better than one,

and because he was capable of abstraction
they were sure he felt a loneliness
deeper than Andrew's, who seemed to know
little more than the discomfort

of every day being himself, a misery
the parents could see on his face.
Often, at breakfast, the parents would
give them a choice—oatmeal or eggs.

If both would say "eggs," John meant
over easy, Andrew, scrambled,
and if ever their plates got mixed up,
Andrew wouldn't eat, while John

would display the look of a child
profoundly misunderstood.
They died at age six, minutes apart,
before certain issues involving

a shared penis could become
even more complicated.
The parents felt John had been spared
that other loneliness—theirs—how to grow

older with names for what they didn't have.
And Andrew, who lived a minute longer,
must have experienced, they thought,
what a flower does when someone picks

the more handsome one right next to it—
some mixture of sadness and what-is-this-
that's-no-longer-here, what-is-this-I'm-feeling?

THE CHICKEN AND THE EGG

The chicken for dinner with earnest friends, the egg for breakfast
with folks who like to play with their food before they eat it.

The chicken fills you up so you can't move,
The egg cracks open, and choices begin—

scrambled, sunny-side up, Benedict . . . Throw in peppers,
cheese, slices of onion, and you have an omelette.

One good, narrow pleasure for the ethicist.
many pleasures for the omelette maker.

The ethicist can't help thinking of Benedict Arnold,
the egg—of Ben, Benjamin, Benny, the varieties

that emerge all gooey, shapeless, to be fooled with.
Yet sometimes the chicken is both necessary and sufficient,

and sometimes your earnest friends instruct you
about how to live with the beak and the gizzard.

The egg allows itself to be hard-boiled or deviled.
It doesn't worry. To live right isn't an issue.

DELICACIES

You can walk a long time
among oaks and pines
before you realize small animals
have been watching you
from their hideaways,
recording, for the good
of their species, how you move,
and what you might do next.

And it's rare when the wind
in the leaves reminds you
of the laughter you heard
one day, far off, the kind
you wanted to move toward,
so devoid of malice, joyous,
at no one's expense.

And even rarer, when out
looking for raspberries,
to come across a bra
on the ground, other articles
of clothing voluntarily—
you're sure—strewn about,

and be moved to turn
and go back to your car
with its tank full of supreme,
quite certain you don't need
to disturb what's sufficient
to imagine or dream.

Testimony

The Lord woke me in the middle of the night,
and there stood Jesus with a huge tray,
and the tray was heaped with cookies,
and He said, Stephen, have a cookie,

and that's when I knew for sure the Lord
is the real deal, the Man of all men,
because at that very moment
I was thinking of cookies, Vanilla Wafers

to be exact, and there were two
Vanilla Wafers in among the chocolate
chips and the lemon ices, and one
had a big S on it, and I knew it was for me,

and Jesus took it off the tray and put it
in my mouth, as if He were giving me
communication, or whatever they call it.
Then He said, Have another,

and I tell you I thought a long time before I
refused, because I knew it was a test
to see if I were a Christian, which means
a man like Christ, not a big ole hog.

THE MAN WITH THREE HORSES

The man with three horses
preferred to ride Big Boy,
the stallion, his favorite.
He admired the palomino's
blond mane, and the musical alto
of her whinny, but she was high
maintenance, and the man
had to work hard to please her.

The third horse wasn't a horse,
but a mule, sure-footed and old
and a little mean. The man,
for some reason, would tell
everybody that he owned
three horses. When someone
would remark, "That one there
looks like a mule," the man simply
would agree, without explanation.

The mule ruled the stable.
The stallion was seventeen hands,
yet a chicken, often spooked
by his own shadow. The palomino
was vain and therefore vulnerable,
given to moodiness if she were not
stroked and brushed every day.

The mule the man called a horse
knew weakness when he saw it,
in fact committed it to memory.

Meanwhile, each day the man
saddled Big Boy
and rode farther and farther
beyond his property.
He didn't want to think
about pecking orders,
or that curious mule, or a palomino
who so lived for admiration
that her presence was exhausting.

None of this bothered the mule.
The man's eccentricities
and the instability of the stable
only served to solidify its power.
And so sure was this mule
of its mulenesss

it would bear whatever burden
the man asked of it.
It would even answer to *horse*
as if it sensed that in this world
or any other, a thing that wasn't
what its name was
had some kind of advantage.

OLD PAST, NEAR PAST

Unsure of who we were
and often too close to a life
of fresh-faced good cheer,
we tried to add complication
to the cleanliness of our reputations—
you, by taking the Greyhound
out of Port Authority amid snow

and wind, heading west, telling no one
what you were doing, not even
your roommate or parents. Me,
falling for a woman
whose violent husband
would soon get out of prison.

And now, this late in our lives,
as we try to account
for the ways each of us
was ready for the other, I think
of you boarding that bus

with just a change of underwear
in your book bag, and a fifty Scotch-taped
to your thigh, and hear it coincide
with some things I'd only dared to dream.

And when I told you about the abortionist
in Brooklyn, and the angel my grandmother
became one desperate night, I wanted you
simply, but not so simply, to know
how far I'd go for love.

Then in those years after our divorces,
how sweet of you (for my sake)
to leave out for as long as you could
your Jeffs and godforsaken Bucks,
and for me, likewise, my Betsys

and that unforgivable Darlene—
all our romances told broadly
until one of us, furious at some small thing,
was tempted to describe that night in Omaha
or Toledo with crazy, nostalgic,
naming-of-names details, but didn't,

only mentioned names, and got names
in return. Later, in bed, the air was rife
with what we'd omitted. Bodies appeared,
and who can sleep well after that, the near
past so close, full of imaginings.

PEDAGOGICAL

In a history paper in college I said the period
between the tsars and Leninism
was a period of transition, and my professor
wrote in the margin, "All periods in history
are periods of transition." I learned nothing
from that, except that he was a wiseguy,
a show-off, someone I would not take again.

Two years later, in a course that focused on Stalin
called The History of Power, I wrote
passionately and I thought persuasively
that much of what he'd done was "inhuman."
In the margin, the response that may be the beginning
of my intellectual life: "Stephen, when it comes
to things like that, *human* will do just fine."

For my Son

after Weldon Kees

To marry Alison, Robert, will be to haul water
from a deep well for the rest of your life.
It will be to worry about beauty
instead of enjoying it. Strange men
are likely to be calling in the middle
of the night. You love her soul, you say,
but Robert, a soul is unmapped territory,
an adventure, and, Alison, trust me,
is a great soul and an adventure
you won't come back from the same.
You're not afraid of change, you say.
Well, you'll have to learn a new language,
hers, which she expects to be understood
before it's spoken. And she'll expect you
to enter a jungle with a fondness
for creatures that can rip you apart.
You're not afraid, you say again. Okay,
appreciate her, she's fabulous, but know
she can't balance a checkbook,
and her desires range from expensive ova
to cuttlebones and chowder. Robert,
no one can make a marriage or the world
behave as he wishes, and I won't
be a broker for what's so breakable.
I just try to make things that last.
I've made you up; I've given you a chance.

OUT OF RESPECT

Donald Justice (1925–2004)

You died many years ago in Miami
on a normal sunny day in the manner
of Vallejo—a death made of words.
The gravedigger spat, and turned away
abruptly, out of respect. As you preferred,
all the conditions were yours.

Now, you're gone for real
in Iowa City, the weather irrelevant,
unimprovable. You've entered the realm
of those beautiful nostalgias you worked
so carefully to make your own.
Out of respect, I shed no tears for you,

who hated tears, you who once said
to a woman who came up to the podium
to say she was moved by your poems,
"I'm sorry you feel that way, Ma'am,
I was after other things."
Oh you were a charming, difficult man.

After the news came, I took your *Selected*
from the shelf, and there you were
again, master of the stilled life
and its tones, and everywhere the tact
of those rich refusals—what you held back,
no doubt out of respect for us.

FEATHERS

If a lone feather fell from the sky,
like a paper plane wafting down
from a tree house where a quiet boy
has been known to hide,
you might think message or perhaps
mischief, not just some mid-air
molting of a bird.
But what if many feathers fell
from a place seemingly higher
than any boy could ever climb,
beyond the top of Savage Mountain
and obscured by clouds,
what might you think then?
A flock of birds smithereened
by hunters? By a jet?
And let's say the feathers were large
and grayish, some of them bloody,
with signs of tendon and muscle
broken off, would you worry about
a resurgence of enormous raptors
only the Air Force knew of,
and had decided to destroy?
For years now you'd heard rumors
of homeless gods in the vast emptiness.
And if they'd appear in your dreams,
as they sometimes did,
begging to be believed in once again,
you'd feel this icy refusal hardening in you.

And when you woke you'd feel it, too.
Your better self wished to believe
the feathers signaled a parade, an occasion
of a triumph, and what was falling
might be a new kind of confetti,
but what was there to celebrate?
Was the world, as you knew it, simply over,
no more rain or snow? Would there always be
just this strange detritus coming down,
covering what used to be the ground?

IV

A Coldness

I don't know if it's a coldness
or just how the body, overloaded,
tends to shut down,
but as my brother neared death
I felt nothing that resembled grief.
Our unfinished business
finished long ago, our love
for each other spoken and real,
there wasn't much more to say
but goodbye, and one morning
we said it—a small moment—
and one of us cried.
From then on he was delusional,
the cancer making him
stupid, insistently so, and lost.
I wanted him to die.
And I wished his wife
would say *A shame*
instead of *God's will*. Or if God
had such a will, *Shame on Him*.
Days later, at the viewing,
again I wanted to feel something,
but for whom? That powdered stranger
lying there, that nobody I knew?
I was far away, parsing grief,
turning it over in my mind.
He was simply gone, a dead thing,
anybody's sack of bones.

Only when his son spoke,
measuring with precise, slow-
to-arrive language the father
he had lost, did something in me move.
There was my brother restored,
abstracted, made of words now.

LETTER TO THE MAN I ONCE WAS

Let's say the place where you wish to belong
won't have you, and the nights turn
charcoal, the heat they once engendered
just a darkness now, an absence really,
and you can only talk to your friends
about privation, which means
gradually they won't want you either—
if it came to this, would you
turn away to mope and snivel, or continue
to imagine conversations getting exciting,
sometimes even fiery and brilliant
in the place that won't have you?

And if there's a middle ground
between the actual and the desirable,
can someone like you find it,
and if you could would you consider
it, by definition, bland, dreamless,
and therefore one of those clubs
you wouldn't enter because it accepted you?

And let's say it's true that loving
makes a place for love, opens you
to the frightening possibilities of joy,
and you also know that most romances
are fraught with failure, would you walk
down that aisle anyway? Or would you
continue to live as if there's always

a better elsewhere, a more dazzling partner?
What logic, if logic is to be followed,
would you follow? Will a cold cup of worry
and a spoonful of dread give you more
comfort, better ease you into the evening?

THE PARTY TO WHICH YOU ARE NOT INVITED

You walk in, your clothes dark
and strangely appropriate, an arrogance
about you as if you had a ramrod
for a spine. You feel posture perfect.

When you speak, women move away.
You smile, and men see tombstones.
They think they know who you are,
that they could throw you out

as they could one man. But today you are
every man who has been omitted
from any list; how quickly they see
they would have no chance.

You pour yourself a drink,
as if ready to become one of them.
Under your skin, nerve endings, loose
wires, almost perceivable. Something

somewhere is burning. You tell them
you've dreamed of moments like this,
to be in their lovely house,
to have everyone's attention. You ask

of the childen, are they napping?
You extend your hand to the host
who won't take it, reminds you
you were not invited, never will be.

You have things in your pockets
for everybody. House gifts.
Soon you'll give them out.
If only they could understand

how you could be ruined
by kindness, how much
you could love them
if they knew how to stop you.

THE PROLIFERATION

Even while we appeared to be
right there in the living room,
we were always looking in

    as if outside
with a telescope—and there it was,
exposed, a certain kind of domesticity.

Yes, a light shone in the darkness,
but the darkness did not comprehend it,
thought of itself as only being itself,

    so self-absorbed
it was sure it covered up everything.
If it recognized the light at all,

it was the way an executioner
might recognize the vein
he was to put the needle in—

    just a little thing
that could be entered
to produce more darkness.

    Inside the house,
a family gathered near the light,
an upright lamp by the sofa.

They saw signs of hope,
they said. One spoke of love,
another of history and its cycles.

But from where we were, we could see
different patterns—years of our parents
in the kitchen, in the bedroom,

and, around them, the proliferation
of darkness. We could see ourselves
in the future.

Oh darkness, you son of a bitch,
we wanted to say, you take-over artist,
how you inform us.

MAGGIE AND THE GAUCHOS

It seemed that from nowhere they came,
their Gaucho jackets flying the flags
of other towns: Rego Park. Corona.

From nowhere, quite suddenly, tire irons
and zip guns replaced fists and language.
We knew their ways wouldn't give
way to anything but confrontation—

we the bookish, we the quiet.
Certain ground had to be held,
somehow defended, the movies
told us, no point in negotiating.

We were fifteen, sixteen, cruisin',
they said, for a bruisin' if we walked
wrong or got in their way.

Maggie, pretty like Natalie Wood,
smart like Stanwyck or Kerr,
could talk with Angelo, leader of the Gauchos,
as easily as with Aaron, our ambassador

of weakness. But they were the Gauchos,
had taken blood oaths, passed initiations.
Their inclination to hurt was monumental.

Those of us vested in the art of cowardice
walked the neighborhood alertly,
usually safe if Maggie walked with us.

It was 1956. Our parents hoped the freedom fighters
in Hungary wouldn't yield to the bully.
They yielded. So little did any of us know
about power, we thought it a failure of nerve.

When my friend Al was attacked
in the alley behind Mama Sorrento's,
Maggie tried to intercede, was pushed

aside, and we learned what the world
would continue to teach us: turf trumps
beauty and smarts, at least in the short run.

I don't know where Maggie is, or what
she did after her stint in the Peace Corps.
I know Angelo died in a knife fight.
Corona has become gentrified.

Artists live there now, but it's America,
and some, I'm sure, keep pistols
under their pillows. The Gauchos have taken

their places in industry and petty crime,
and in my recurring dream
meet their proper deaths time after time.

THE WIDENING

I was holding forth at the dinner table,
trying to fill what I perceived to be a void.
I had just read a book on music,
about which I know very little,
and, anticipating being corrected, was saying
something about the courage to have
a full stop, the courage to break off,
the breaking of rhythmic obligations.

Then the phone rang: my daughter's lost cat
had been found. I told everyone, and the void
seemed to fill a little with good cheer,
like vodka at the bottom of a glass.

So I told them that the baby crow
a hawk had tried to kill this morning
was still alive—three birds of different species
standing around it as if on guard.

The hawk was up on a nearby branch,
frowning, I said. No one smiled or laughed.

But we were mostly a dour group,
long neglected reciprocity dinners
finally acted upon, payback time,
and the social scientists among us—
who wouldn't know a good story
unless research confirmed it good—

wanted me to name the three species.
Flu fly, plutark, Dickey do—I couldn't
help myself—and the void widened again.

I wanted to go home, but I was home.

How about the hawk, my friend
Bjorn, the clarinetist, said,
and the hungers of the strong?
And by the way, he added,
there's no such thing as a full stop
in music—silence is a sound, an afterlife
for anyone with an ear.

I'd like to say I felt corrected, not betrayed,
and when I began to talk about miracles
and the Bee Gees singing "Stayin' Alive"
and Travolta being reborn before our eyes,
I'd like to say I didn't know why.

Actually, I did, and didn't
want to say my mind had drifted
from music and obligations
to baseball, the beautiful choreography
of its dreams and errors. I wanted to say
that with some good stops at the right time
and some luck it's possible to survive.

I wanted to tell them that in my ignorance
I was serious, and that when things get lost
or are about to die all kinds of thoughts are legitimate.
It was my house, after all, and the floor was mine.

ODDS ARE

If you find yourself on a long streak of good luck,
when even the sloth in you is awarded best in class,
and then a horse with your name and your money

wins by a nose, you might think you don't need
anyone to suggest that you take stock, look around.
Nor are you likely to see the shadowy, unguaranteed

future hiding right there in the open. You'll just want
to roll the dice, keep it all going.
If a stranger passing by, says, *Watch out, brother,*

maybe for a moment, but only a moment, you'll be jolted
into the prurience of your self-regard
before you curse and dismiss him. And when

you shop the organics aisle hoping to meet thin women,
you'll not be daunted when no one responds
to your cart full of proteins and carbs.

Take it on faith, or from the suddenly visible world:
odds are you'll still need another sign
that luck has gone to someone else's side.

THE OBVIOUS

Sometimes when the obvious is out there
battling to get past its lightweight reputation
and offer us what it conceals,

little apertures appear, invite the eye.
A man can see his wife readying herself
to say goodbye; another sees himself

hiding behind his photographs
of achievement, a tiny replica of a man
up on the mantel with his victories.

Of course, others have noticed these things
for months, years. But how nice, sometimes,
not to see the storm coming and blithely walk

into it, singing. How nice when we survive
our blindness, our stupidities,
and manage to get rewarded.

Yet the obvious is dangerously everywhere,
part of the daily mask and façade.
Sometimes it stares back at us, in disbelief

that we haven't seen that rose or AK-47.
Sometimes it just taps us on the shoulder,
revealing what only to us is a revelation.

ACHE

"I want to help you," a stranger wrote,
"with your infernal ache,"
as if he knew something I didn't.
He called me "friend," as so many do
these days, without affection
or permission. "The light you create
must be like no other," he went on
to say, "let me be of assistance."
Turns out he was a guy selling drugs,
smart enough to know aches
are ubiquitous, and can feel infernal.
Write to a thousand, hook one.
He was easy to delete.
But all day I thought of what must be
his successes, and wondered how often
that one person—alone, with a cat
on her lap and the cane
she uses to help herself rise
and get to the kitchen and back—
answers him, thinking, Who else
knows me so well, or cares so much?

FOR THE PLAYER

You can't write music right unless you
know how the man that's gonna play it,
plays poker.
                                    —Duke Ellington

Every day is a first day, you need
to believe, if you wish to astonish.
There it is, the world—try to look at it

coldly, see behind its glamor
and gloom, hear it, read it
the way good poker players do—

this bravado, that tic, a movement
of hand to ear—the whole table,
over time, revealing itself.

No booze for a while.
A good drinking song
never gets written by a drunk.

Have your martinis chilled
with two olives, but after you close
shop, when everything is yours.

That's the time to talk,
shoot the shit, as Ellington
might say, elegant as he was.

Don't come knocking at a door
unless you have a gift.
Beauty helps, but isn't enough—

flowers don't grow
in hopes of ending up in a vase.
Offer something you can do

more right than anyone else.
If it's sexy
it's wise to also make it sad.

If you're pushing freedom,
Ellington once said,
you'd better love constraint.

In Another Country

The merchants of solace are out tonight
hawking their antidotes
for this or for that, and you think
you're smart enough not to yield.
Soon, though, you'll be caught up
in the vortex of a strange compulsion,
pulled into the spectacle-life
of a visitor in a foreign country.
You'll want what you don't want
because the smells are new,
the murmurs in the market apparently
sounds of satisfaction. But take up
residence, and it's all likely to fall apart,
almost everything that feels exalted
weakened by time. Her eyes will lose
their luster, his charm will mark him
as unambitious, the colorful garments
the natives wear will seem showy, foppish.
You buy the stuffed lizard for your son
because you know a bargain when you see one.
You'd buy menace if it were on sale.
The promiscuous always gives you pleasure
before a certain melancholy sets in.
The truth is you've never been smart enough
not to yield, especially in places
where the dancers click their heels
and dinner begins long after dark. You're
an American. You were born to be pleased.
Somewhere it says so.

The Statue of Responsibility

Imagine it's given to us as a gift
from a country wishing to overcome its own hypocrisy.
I can see someone standing up at a meeting
and saying, Give it to the Americans, they like
big things for their people, they like to live
in the glamor between exaltation and anxiety.
Instead of an arm raised with a torch, let's insist
they cement its feet deep into the earth, burden it
with gigantic shoes—an emblem of the inescapable.

We place it on land, across from Liberty
on the Brooklyn side. And I can see myself needing
to visit it regularly, taking the elevator up
to its chest area where I'd feel something
was asked of me. Near its heart, I'd paint
After the tyrants, there's nothing as hateful
as the martyrs. And I'd stare at those words,
trying to understand my motive to enlighten
by desecration.

In one of its enormous feet, I imagine a gift shop
where tourists can buy replicas
of Responsibility for themselves and friends
they think might need it. And I'd want
bumper stickers selling for almost nothing:
Less talk of conscience, more of consciousness.

I can see my friend, the ex–altar boy,
for so long injured by memory, writing
near the statue's eyes, *See everything;*
overlook a great deal; correct a little—
then scratching jagged lines through
that wisdom of Pope John XIII.
clearly now irresponsible. And yet his words
remain ones I'd like to live by.
How to defend that? How to decide?

SEA LEVEL

Down from the mountains of Appalachia
and the highs of new love
I've come across the extended monotonies
of interstates, back to where
scrub pines stand small at sea level.
There's the house I left for good
(if forever can ever be good),
and there's the Great Egg Harbor River,
which widens here, and everywhere
the visages of ghosts appear
and disappear. I've come to visit
the friends who've stayed
casualty's course—the dearest ones,
who somehow have learned to live
amid the messiness of allegiances,
the turns and half turns of whom now
to console, whom to embrace, and when.
I pull into their driveway, wanting
to tell them how it feels to have—
for the first time—an undivided heart,
a sudden purity of motive,
but when I begin to speak I realize
I don't. I say it anyway, won't take it
back. When their outside cat wants in,
they let him in. Then he wants out.
They accommodate. That cat
is almost as lucky as I. No mountains

here, I can see the afternoon sun
on the horizon hanging on,
about to dip and be gone. Their yard
is a dusty orange. I love the truth,
I swear I do.